Unveil
From All The Coats
Sing Your Heart

Also by Torry Fountinhead

*The 7 Pillars Your Authentic Self Stands On, Part I of
The Essential Companion Series*

The Beauty, Part I of The Contemplation Series

The Soul's Openner, Part II of The Contemplation Series

*Reach The Fountain Of Youth, Part III of
The Contemplation Series*

*Shush! It's a Secret, The Lake Hides His Dummy, Part
of The Rainbow of Life's Secrets*

*Poem: Good Enough, Part of Forever Spoken,
The International Library of Poetry*

*A Tip of an Iceberg Meditations, a series of short books
among are:*

Is Forgiving a Riddle?
Momentary Thoughts
The Life The Heart Sprouts
For As It Is The Mind That Makes The Body Rich
Unveil From All The Coats, Sing Your Heart
and many more at work…

Unveil
From All The Coats
Sing Your Heart

Part V of "A Tip of an Iceberg Meditations"
Series

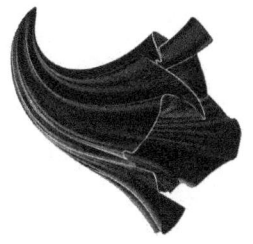

By

Torry Fountinhead

Airé Libré Publishing & Computing Ltd.

eBook ISBNs:
ISBN-10: 0-9733450-4-7
ISBN-13: 978-0- 9733450-4-9
Print Book ISBNs:
ISBN-10: 0-9733450-3-9
ISBN-13: 978-0-9733450-3-2

© 2018 Torry Fountinhead
All Rights of this work are Reserved. No part or whole may be used, copied or reproduced, stored in retrieval systems, or transmitted, in any form or by any means whatsoever, including electronic media, mechanical, photocopying, recording, or otherwise.

For more information contact:
Airé Libré Publishing & Computing Ltd.
Suite 306, 185-911 Yates St.
Victoria BC V8V 4Y9 Canada
Tel: 1-250-592-3099.
http://www.al.bc.ca   info@al.bc.ca

Book Web-Site URLs:
http://unveilfromallthecoats.atipofanicebergmeditations.ca

Part of:
Http://www.atipofanicebergmeditations.ca
Http://www.tipofaniceberg.ca
Http://www.atipofanicebergmeditations.com
Http://www.tipofaniceberg.com

"Denying your Authentic Self significance, and taking on false identities, is like denying your existence."

Torry Fountinhead

Table of Content

Unveil From All The Coats	i
Unveil From All The Coats	iii
Table of Content	vii
Unveil From All The Coats	ix
Prologue	1
I A baby, an Unknown Creation	3
II The Triangular Knowledge Effects	7
III Input	11
IV Who Are You?	15
V Coping With Differences	21
VI This Is The Time To Start Asking	25
VII Define Yourself	29
VIII The Arm's-Length Trick	35
IX Unveiling The False Self	39
X Defining Who You Really Are	49
Oh Mirror	57
XI This which is Success	59
Epilogue	67
Apendicies	69
Apendix I	71
Apendic II	85
A word about this series	87
Notes	89

Unveil
From All The Coats
Sing Your Heart

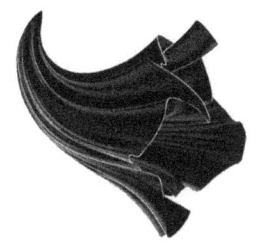

Prologue

Imagine and consider this:

Human Beings are under the *wrong* assumption that a baby is born in a state of 'Tabula Rasa' namely, a clean slate.

This baby, yes, has to learn the immediate information of the specific point in time it has been born to, but it has three significant fountains of knowledge and wisdom within – born with.

Yet, Humanity is out to 'program' this baby, as if it is a brand new computer that has to be 'installed' and 'uploaded' with information, programs, etc.

From the moment of birth, a war has been launched, and carried on throughout the life of this Human Being, the war between being its true Authentic Self, and that which others deem it to be.

The 'size' of the war will be in direct relation to the caregivers' perception, and the environment it was born to.

When, and how, the baby – now grown up, lets go of what is not authentically his – is yet to be seen.

You will be well advised to let go of all that you have heard in comments, judgements, songs, teachings, news, movies, and all forms of input – unveil them from your mind, feelings, and even your soul.

What if, you have taken upon yourself burdens heavy as thick coats, but you are in a tropical zone of existence?

Become that which you have been created to be – your authentic self.

I
A baby, an Unknown Creation

A man and a woman, came together to couple, in an act of surrender, and hopefully, with joy.

They might have wished only to share themselves, but could also have wished to bring forth the act of creating another Human Being.

Within this moment, all that matters is the intention held in each of their minds, as it is loading the moment with possibilities.

The entire composite of the man and

woman, their emotions, state of minds, energy levels, interests, level of equanimity, and much more is loading the moment with vibrational information, to be translated, transmuted, and affecting the act of sharing.

Out of their control, even if they so wished it, a conception might happen, or not. The conception is at the hand of Creation, not of the Human Beings'.

If conception has happened, a new destiny is now to be woven, to join the fabric of their lives.

This moment of entry was preceded by many parameters that were included in the formula, of the coming new being.

Alas, the couple already has some pre-conceived ideas of what to expect. The baby, although totally unknown to them, is also a concept, which is known to them, to a greater degree.

The same couple also has an idea of what they will 'allow', and what not, regarding the demand of the baby on their time, money, attention, and more.

Yet, whether the child is healthy, or not, a Mozart re-incarnation, or ordinary, it will fall into their 'expectations', and habitual way of thinking.

There are so many details that we are not aware of, from our vantage point, here on Earth, as Human Beings. Society is limited in its ability to give absolute answers to this unknown,

Therefore, it is to our Higher Selves that we should look to, for guidance.

Unveil From All The Coats - Sing Your Heart

II
The Triangular Knowledge Effects

The trilateral knowledge factor is born out of all that is involved.

Although, a foetus is usually started just by an egg and a sperm that become the initial cell that is to divide endlessly until, a full mature foetus is ready to be born; this initial cell has consciousness already, as well as each cell to come would have.

This consciousness is born of the intention of creation, and has all the knowledge of how to survive, multiply, and evolve. I am sure that you are aware that cells develop to be different parts of the body. We also know that the new creation has the spiritual undefinable part.

In addition to the consciousness, this cell already carries the DNA information from both parents. Within this DNA, not only do we find the particulars that will determine the physicality of the baby-to-come, but we also find some transferable knowledge.

You can recognise this knowledge within some examples, for instance, where the generations of the late 19th, and early 20th centuries knew how to calculate arithmetic, they did not know how to use an electronic calculator, but when it came available, they have learnt, as it became necessary.

Their children, and grandchildren, did not have any problem whatsoever in learning how to operate it, in a lightning speed, as well as transfer this knowledge to new electronic devices, as they became available.

You see, all ideas, and knowledge, are enriching the Universal Consciousness and thus, becomes accessible to all.

Alas, another type of knowledge is transferred with the DNA, and it is the common reactionary behavioural of the parents, and their ancestors before them. This also includes the species traits, e.g., the fight or flight survival mechanism.

It is not widely known from what point the foundational psychology of the baby starts, but foetuses exhibit character traits, behavioural traits, preferences, and temper, right at the foetus stage, and long before birth.

A side note of interest would be that maybe that was one of the causes, our ancestors wanted to attach astrological characteristics to people, as it was obvious that babies already exhibited their own character, and the parents wanted to attribute it to the influence of the stars versus, their own makeup while, it could actually be both.

The third type of knowledge is obtained during the months of pregnancy while, the foetus, (and all consciousness involved and present,) feels emotions, environmental states and changes, hears, and exposed to multitude of things.

Surely, you have noticed how sensitive the baby's skin is, in addition to its hearing, and so on.

All these impressions cause many things,

not in the least are belief systems, and worst of all – fears, and confusions.

Our baby then, as you may ascertain, is a bundle of knowledge right from the start, and not only a bundle of joy.

If parents would take this into consideration, they would practice far more diligence in acknowledging their part, and responsibilities, in this creational act.

III
Input

The three types of knowledge, discussed in the previous chapter, are important to consider, as a fertile soil that all additional inputs are falling upon, and enhance, cement, and further define their details.

Inputs are all things that we are exposed to, willingly or not. Some are good, as they help us grow, mature, and evolve, but some are not so.

In the 2nd part of the 20th century, when television became the new mode of entertainment, and communication, a new habit has emerged, parents started to put their babies in front of the TV, in order to keep them engaged therefore, not crying, or demanding attention.

All that was shown on TV therefore, becomes input registered by the baby's mind, without any ability to determine if it was good, or not.

The baby's brain, and most importantly the front lobe that facilitates common sense, is not fully developed, and will not be, for that matter, not up until the approximate age of 21.

Conditionings not only started to be established while in vitro, but now also continue via the use of false informational modes. It does not only happen by audio and video inputs, but also by the spoken and non-spoken emotions, behaviours, opinions, and facial expressions, etc. of the people surrounding this baby – family, and out there on the street.

All of this, even before considering the 'treatment' the baby actually receives from one, and all.

The treatment of the baby is also a measurement of, and creator of, the 'norm' the baby uses as a point of reference throughout its life to be.

This baby develops multiple Mind-sets, as per the 'condition' it is in, the 'environment', which people surround him, and where does it go, because the most important and basic mind-set is of survival.

Thereafter, the 'programming' starts, whether at home, kindergarten, school, or extra-curricular activities. May it be the programming dictated by the government, the educational system, specific teachers, instructors, caregivers, or even peers.

If you take the observer's position, and look at this foetus – becoming a baby – becoming a growing child to adult, you might be able to see how many layers of information have been laid upon this person, layers that could be construed as burdens.

It is important to acknowledge that our brain, as the receiver and interpreter of all signals coming towards us, is not the only receiver mechanism within our being, but all are bombarded with endless input – seen or unseen, heard or unheard, felt or unfelt, perceived or not.

IV
Who Are You?

Actually, one should ask Who Am I?

While, many people have heard in their life the question: whom do you think you are (…asking xyz), in actuality, we have a situation of trying to discern who we really are, because of that 'war' I referred to in the Prologue.

Human babies are born entirely depended

on their caregivers, so although they register everything, they are not yet in a position to express themselves verbally.

The portions of the brain that will facilitate future verbal communication are to be further developed, and so is the vocabulary. In the meantime, the baby expresses itself, as best as possible, by using subtle, and not so subtle, means.

I mention the 'subtle', because it is a key to understand your baby. Watch their eyes, and the rest of their body language, and you will see what I mean.

Somewhere around the age of six months, the baby will be able to distinguish better that it is a separate being than its immediate caregiver. Its own opinions will also start to form, rightly, or wrongly, but for sure, according to its own character coupled with the previous conditionings.

Further to the fact that the primary requirement is survival, one may observe that the baby behaviours are as per the demands of the circumstances.

The baby does not know yet that there is a difference between the known, and the unknown. It only knows that each circumstance allows it certain freedom, which it then takes, and 'run with.'

When we refer to a child as 'pushing his luck', in actuality we say that the child 'over shot' the boundaries we have set for it, to start-off with.

The baby, and then child, is trying to find a way, not only to 'survive', but also to express itself 'safely', diminishing any scolding, pain, and or fear inducing responses.

It is in self-expression that the child finds the courage to 'sound his voice.' A voice that he has since conception, but that has to be exercised in order to be clear.

One may ask why it is all right for a singer to repeatedly practice their voice, but not to you and me – and the baby.

The thoughts that are running in everybody's mind are many and varied, but they are certainly formed differently when expressed verbally. Whether in speech, or writing, once you form the thoughts, you have a chance to form the picture of the idea you hold in mind.

The child tries to do exactly that. It tries to bring forth a definition to the conceptual idea it has in mind.

This may also be demonstrated by painting artists. Their painting is of a specific idea, even if the idea was just to cement a beautiful view that touched their heart, for posterity.

Many of the fairy tales, and children stories, demonstrate how trial-and-error, or believing the wrong person, innocence versus deceit, utopian happiness, and or holding onto your dreams and believing in yourself, are necessary to put into words possible scenarios.

All that we are 'trying' to do is equip the child with some yardsticks of reference. Alas, we do much more while we are in the process of educating it, not in the least, confirming with our opinions that these are the 'true' yardsticks.

It is true that the baby might not be able to *define* their own tastes in the beginning, but that does not give us an authorisation to force our tastes on it.

How do we expect the baby to develop well, if we place so many hurdles on its way?

Yet another side note, do you think that so many people, during the 19th through the 21st centuries, would have needed psychoanalysis, where guiding, coaching, and steering, made by a wise, patient, and loving elder could have had a much better result, and would have promoted true personal growth.

Adults would be wise to adopt the 'pause' mechanism namely, instead of looking at what is happening, and immediately relating to it as a problem that has to be solved right now – Pause and Breath. See if the best solution is already at hand, and or allow the baby maybe to come up with its own solution and thus, teach the baby self-reliance, promote his efforts for inventiveness, and encourage him for independence.

Unveil From All The Coats - Sing Your Heart

V
Coping With Differences

Initially, the baby, as mentioned before regarding the multiple mind-sets it will conjure, will try to flow with the situation at hand.

It will try to understand and cope with the feelings, and the unspoken signals that it gets, by moulding into what is the least dangerous for its survival.

The inner knowing already exists, and when you will find a baby rebelling, and or showing forceful indignation, you would know that what it is going through is against its grain, *and it is courageous enough to display it.*

Alas, there are some babies who will withdraw their responses, and become either tremendously quiet, or introspective , before or after trying to express themselves first.

This is only the initial behaviour. Later on, some babies will try to exert their influence by 'acting up', and some by finding their own way, quietly.

The nature of a young Human Being is inquisitive, joyful, laughing, and interested. Similar to every growing plant that seeks the warmth of the sun, and the direction of growth.

If you find that the baby, or child, is not showing all of these characteristics, it is there where you must start your investigation to the anomalies in its life.

No doubt that there are some babies, that by the definition of their own character, will require encouragement, and or enticing, but even they will show the same natures, mentioned above, only in a more of a shy way.

I witnessed many variations on the theme while watching many babies. You see – I love their acknowledging look, and thankful if I am rewarded with a genuine smile.

There is something to say about how of a narrow-vision our lives are. We are not only born to certain circumstances that dictate the majority of our 'allowed' behaviour, and expectations. Not only are we born to figures of authority in our young lives, which allow us, or not, to develop naturally. We are also confined, initially, to our five senses for learning the world around us.

A baby still feels the connection to that which it came from, but is bound to the physical life – trying to make sense of it – and survive.

How else would one explain the existence of fear, complacency, shyness, lack of motivation, and myriad of other inflictions that stump us so powerfully?

Human Beings are taught that they have been fashioned of clay by the Creator; alas, our babies are *not* clay in *our* hands. Our babies are not to be fashioned by *us*, as we deem fit for them to be. We are given the honour of *caring* for a soul that was born into a body, in the manner of parenthood, without any mandate of 'completing their creation'.

Our babies born complete, they only go through learning and evolving, in this 'school of Earth'.

In the name of this chapter, I used the word 'coping', as to illustrate that the survival issue in our lives is far higher in priority, to that of striving. Otherwise, I could have used the word 'overcoming', which requires us to look at the content of our next chapter.

VI
This Is The Time To Start Asking

A question, not necessarily only asking 'why', but also 'how come', 'how could it be', 'am I mystified', 'am I confused – and if yes, why', are just some of the questions that are building up a mountain in front of our awareness' door.

The time, when we find this mountain to be so large that we cannot avoid it any longer, could be early or later in the process of life, and is unavoidable.

We are all born with the power of choice – with free will. Therefore, it is easy to discern when and how we are being 'dictated to'.

Sometimes we think it might be 'safe' to accept our community belief systems, habits, and instructions, in other words, follow the majority while, us, is a minority of one. How dare we?

William Shakespeare once said that "One touch of nature makes the whole world kin" – and we might have mistaken 'kin' to cancel our right to be singular, and unique. Even in a catastrophe, although communities will get together to act as one, to save the many – it is still a conglomeration of many singulars that build the unity, the efforts of each one count towards the action, as a whole.

This brings to mind the unison, in which a flock of birds may fly, like the Starlings, all performing their dance in unison. This bird-unison is born out of their connection to the group consciousness, and therefore, allows them to act as one, with no delay.

I actually suspect that this bird-unison might explain another phenomenon namely, and as an example, towards the evening, when the Robin sings its evening song. Although you might have a large group of Robins in the immediate vicinity, only one sings – one may attribute it to 'the one that sings for all – or actually for the whole', as we do not even hear them sing as a choir.

I once wrote, "Dare something worthy of your love and dedication, dare to have the courage to pursue it to completion and thus, follow your heart, and you have in your mind a righteous mission."

You may recognise in this, the inclusion of a number of aspects that are required in order to be able to 'dare'. All of which are aspects that you may derive to via self-questioning.

In order to recognise that you 'love' something, you have to be aware.

In order to be 'dedicated', you have to have values that will support you in choosing what to dedicate yourself to.

In order to have 'courage', you have to know yourself enough. To know what you are apprehensive of, what previously might have stopped you in your tracks, and then really know the importance of that that you would like to accomplish, or pursue, take a deep breath – and go onwards.

In order to 'follow' your heart, you will have to be truthful to yourself, acknowledge your inner clarity, and imbue your goal with your love, to strengthen yourself on the way.

The result of knowing yourself, being truthful to yourself, loving, being dedicated, and being courageous, connects you to your true self, who is always good – as we are all created good, the non-positive of life stems from reasons that manifested after our creation, and is not part of our true makeup. Therefore, in your mind then, you can only have a righteous mission that will benefit the highest good of all, including yourself.

In my book, The Soul Openner, I coined a phrase saying, "If you believe your destination, you become your goal". In order to become your goal, the need to define yourself will stem from your efforts to know yourself truly.

Therefore, you would be able to Dare Something Worthy.

VII
Define Yourself

In 'defining yourself' I mean – find your own true identity, that which is uniquely you, and although it might be similar to another – it is no one else's.

I mentioned earlier that each cell in our body has a consciousness, yet, they are all supporting the being that is you. This support is born of the idea of your own identity that the cells respond to.

In nature and within us too, collaboration is the true basis, and not competition. Therefore, the cells of our body recognise their existence within the being that is you and thus, aim to work in collaboration for the highest good of this being.

When you maintain a solid identity of yourself, with awareness and intention, and do not adopt other's identity, the cells of your body can identify you. If, on the other hand, your identity is compromised, because of either stress, or choice, disease may set in – as inharmonious condition exists within.

Disease may also manifest as a result of other causes, but when your unique identity is coherent within all cells of your body, it would be easier for your body to respond with spontaneous healing. Otherwise, it would need further help.

Maybe one may contemplate also the seeming puzzle in our language namely, look at the following two words, and their meaning:

Illness – looked at as I-llness, and

Wellness – looked at as WE-llness.

When all the cells of the body relate to one another, knowing your identity, and working in collaboration, you get the 'WE' factor, which leads to Wellness.

When a cell is self-oriented, and disregard the other cells, and your identity, it works for itself, not unlike cancer cells, and brings in the 'I' factor, and thus, Illness.

I could also use the analogy of the sea, or river. Each drop of water within the sea is part of the whole body of the sea, and moves as part of the whole. It is only when the sea hits upon rocks, or reacts to wind, that you may see the water part, in many ways.

Throw a pebble into a pond, and it is clear how the calm, seemingly unified water, break and respond with ripples.

Yet again, as I mentioned in Chapter II, we are a conglomeration of many consciousness units. What unites us is our *distinct* identity.

'Distinct' versus a collection of identities, this is why it is so important for us *not* to adopt other people's identity, or even imitate another, just because we want to 'copy' their success etc. (see chapter XI This Which is Success for more.)

Although we are part of the whole of Humanity, we are not meant to act as one – or even like a herd. Human Being are born to have different experiences, different outlooks, and be the different aspects of the diamond, shining the light, that is Humanity.

Otherwise, how can we bring forth, share, and enlarge the experiential knowledge and wisdom that feeds Humanity whole group-consciousness.

Sentient beings, which we are part of, are going through a *personal* evolution that comprises several stages and cycles. We may only evolve for and by ourselves; we can only proceed on our own journey – by ourselves.

If, and when, you will take the time, regularly, to look within, you will find an immense ocean of knowing, of inspiration, of innate wisdom, and much more.

Some of what you will find will be similar across all Human Beings, but a lot will be different. I could even joke and say that the reason there are so many Chefs, of so many cuisines in the world, is that a one singular taste *would never satisfy all* Human Beings.

Look even at fashion, it keeps changing,

may it be cloths, computers, electronics, music genres, musicians, art, artists, it does not matter which.

In Life, *change* is the name of the game – and this is the reason why it is so important to have a solid foundation – your own rock to lean on – ***your own unified and distinct identity.***

Do not be afraid to discover who you are, even if in your outer world you meet with no appreciation. You are born good. You are born free. You are born with free will – the power of choice.

Others might try to tell you that it is not so, but they are not 'the final authority' of Creation, they just voice their opinions that sometimes might be even mean.

On you journey within, you will discover this to be the Truth, so let yourself be empowered by it.

You have the right to be yourself, as long as you do not harm another.

VIII
The Arm's-Length Trick

Imagine yourself twirling with your arms stretched out to your sides and while you turn, a drawing of an invisible circle is drawn around you; its diameter is your arm-stretch's length.

Inwardly, declare that within this circle you are the decision maker, the one that decides who may enter it, and who may not, and for how long they would stay within – you could call it 'your Immediate Sanctuary'.

It is similar to the sub-conscious feeling that you have while driving a car whereby, the car's body actually becomes your conscious-body and thus, you are able to drive without 'scraping' any other vehicle on the road.

Now, draw an outer circle to this one, multiplying the diameter by two, and declare this one to be the 'no-land zone' namely, it is a zone that does not belong to anyone specifically, but may be used to converse, or interact with others.

At the outer edge of this imaginary second larger circle, install an imaginary screen-like sifter, which covers the whole of your height-span almost like a curtain flowing from top to bottom. You could imbue it with a colour, blue, pink, or just white, for example, or a rainbow full of colours. See these colour(s) shimmering – constantly, in your mind's eye.

If, and when, you allow in your mind anyone, or anything, to enter this no-land zone, they will first pass through this shimmering colourful glow, which transmute their intentions towards you, because you have set an intention of a loving welcome towards them and yourself, when you invited them in.

While you converse, or interact, keep a deep awareness on your feelings, and bodily movements, they will be your indicators, as to how 'safe' you are at this moment.

The idea of erecting such circle around yourself is two-fold.

Firstly, your awareness about yourself, and what is going on there, is paramount to your whole health.

Secondly, while being aware, you are taking responsibility over your life, and all that is in it.

The result of which, you would feel far more self-confident, self-sufficient, and loving.

When the idiom "at an arm's length" was conceived, it was after people were hurt – why should we even go there, and more over – unprepared.

Loving other people, and living things, having 'a healthy' concern about them does not imply that it has to be done by cancelling your healthy existence, nor by writing yourself off.

While keeping the arm's length, you can successfully keep your cool, calm and collected demeanour, and thus, act more naturally, and positively, as the occurrence prescribes.

It will give you time to pause, and not force you to react.

It will also allow you to better enjoy your own company, and smile upon Life.

The same may apply to all forms of 'input' that engage your life, anything from the news, to corresponding with loved ones. Social media, to movies, songs, shows, books, and any other information you 'choose' to expose yourself too – remember you do have the power of choice, you do have Free Will.

For those times that you might feel that you were exposed to input not of your choosing, remember that you still have the power of choice of how to respond – what attitude you are going to have to face it with.

This way you may even lead by example namely, children and adults would be able to ascertain, consciously or sub-consciously, that this easy-mannered way is easier, and uplifting.

IX
Unveiling The False Self

Remember the 'coats' I referred to earlier?

Let us go back to the idea that our realm of existence might not be the same, as we think it to be.

With the 'coat', I tried to illustrate an idea that if you are at a tropical zone namely, the temperature is warm and calls for wearing a swimsuit, you would hardly entertain a thought of wearing a heavy fur coat, would you.

Yet, many of us find that we are hardly ever 'dressed' appropriately to the surrounding we find ourselves in.

The analogy really speaks of all the opinions, belief systems, pre-conceived ideas, and prejudices that are within us; only, we are not always the ones that actually instilled it within.

Even our own name may indicate to us some pre-conceived idea.

We could start our way to self-understanding by maybe presenting ourselves with some non-threatening questions, and here are some examples:

When I was conceived, what was my idea about myself – did I have any?

When I was a foetus, did I know who I was?

When I was born, did I know whom I was?

When I saw the faces of my caregivers, did I know who they were?

When I realised that we were not 'one', did I know who I was?

When I realised that we were not 'one', did I know who they were?

When they started to refer to me with one repetitive word, did I realise that that was a name that they have given me?

What did I feel about that name?

Did they tell me that the name symbolised something, or someone?

How did I feel about always reminding them of that someone, every time they called my name?

Did I even think that there was a connection to whom I really was?

When did I start to feel *different*?

Why could I not always understand why I was told 'no'?

Why could I not always understand why certain things were said about me?

Why I do not have the means to express myself clearly?

I guess, by now, you can follow the gist of how questions can start to unveil things about yourself that could just be false – nothing to actually do with you, but very much to do with other people.

If I am really to compose for you *all* the questions, it will take a lifetime to write, and many lifetimes to answer. Therefore, we should look for a short-cut.

Firstly, if you can answer the questions already listed here, your mind will already become comfortable with the idea of self-questioning.

Secondly, you will develop a habit of questioning everything, leaving no idea unturned.

Thirdly, and I do so wish you would, you could find the 'playfulness' with which you could play this questioning game with yourself, as it needs not be painful, but revealing.

If you meet with some answers that might be painful, remember, you did not set it up to start off with, you just accepted something, before you could discern if it was true, or not.

Belief systems are rather 'funny' in that that they do not have to be true at all. They started by a thought that became an opinion, opinion that was repeated enough times to make it sound as if it is so. Many a times, the person holding that belief might not even remember what was the initial thought, and if it ever had any merit.

In the same way are attitudes. We always respond to life with the way we 'are' at that specific moment. Namely, our condition, as well as conditioning, our mental and emotional states, our level of tiredness and nutrition, what were we doing just before and how it affects our plan, our character and traits, all of this, and more, affects our response, and puts us in a place of 'attitude'.

Thank Goodness that we have Free Will, so we may then adjust our attitude to benefit our highest good, and not bring harm to ourselves, or others.

Many years ago, I met someone who was very distressed by what others said about him. I asked whether he believed that what they have said was true, and he answered 'well, of course not'.

I proceeded to ask, what the reason behind his anger was. Was it because he believed it threatened his existence somehow, to which his answer was 'no'.

He thought that they did not have the 'right' to think that way about him.

I then asked with a mischievous grin, 'so if I said that you have a green nose, or a purple one, would you be insulted?'

His immediate answer was 'no, this is ridiculous'.

This is where I drew his attention to the fact that I purposefully chose a ridiculous example, in order to illustrate the difference between what others might think of you, and what the truth is, regardless of the content.

Of course, it is important to check the actual validity of the comments, and opinions, as much as it is important to ascertain if the other person's opinion stems from pain.

Many times, people will react from pain, and or some rather an overwhelming condition, and use rush words.

Are you familiar with the saying 'as water off duck's back'?

Here I am referring to the same idea. First let other people's opinions be said, then, check them as per the truth you hold about yourself.

Secondly, evaluate the opinions, and decide whether you should actually internalise them, or not, but take a moment to acknowledge whether you might already hold the same opinions, or beliefs.

You might be surprised at finding that you already have adopted these opinions, or beliefs, and now they just 'play' in your life, like a broken record.

In reality, do you not think that if your own body regenerate at every moment of your day, and life, that it could just be that the whole of you is 'anew' at every moment?

Is it not safer and more profitable to relate to one self as anew with every choice we make, and with every breath we take?

In reality, we are an unfolding story. We are pacing ourselves on our journey, and sometimes we are fully aware of it.

It is for the times that we move like automatons that we should awake and ask – who is in control?

Although it is cosy to act in familiar ways, on familiar grounds, and not call for our courage before every action – it is really far more natural for us to be versatile, courageous, adventurers, inquisitive, and creative.

Beside, being predictable might be good

when people know that you are reliable, but not when they know exactly how you would respond, or react, in each situation.

This calls for knowing thyself and the values you aspire to, because your reliability, high integrity, and abilities will stem from them, and then you may be free to be the versatile being you were born to be.

It is similar to learning the steps of a dance, or a form in martial arts. Once you know the 'choreography', you can personalise it, embellish it, and use it to *your* full expression.

Unveiling yourself means, going back to your own truth and nature. It means, utilising your gifts and talents versus following another's.

It also mean that because you are dynamic – you may change your mind, you may take a different route, you may act differently – and be loved and appreciated regardless – because your basic 'value' has not changed.

You are valuable from your creation – and not because other people granted you your value!

The movers and the shakers of the world, followed their own star, imagination, and inventiveness, and thus, set for us new and wonderful things. Certainly, they were far truer to themselves then any of their critics.

With the view of unveiling yourself, let us look at how to define yourself – positively.

Unveil From All The Coats - Sing Your Heart

X
Defining Who You Really Are

Surely, you are aware that no one has found two people with the same fingerprints, yet, as well as no two people with the same DNA mapping, even if they were identical twins. If they were found, it would have been a breaking news story, and they would have been listed in the Guinness book of records.

Taking the example of identical twins, you will find that that most of the times, they react differently to foods, chemicals, weather, music genres, and multitude of other things, so even there uniqueness is the rule.

This is the most important starting point namely, *knowing that you are unique.*

When, and not if, you will acknowledge this simple fact that you are unique, you may start listing your traits, gifts, habits, talents, aspirations, and anything of interest, accepting that it is part of your own makeup.

You will also be less self-judgemental, because you will understand that any society's norm, or rule, is made to commonly fitting a large number of people, even if there are some rules, like the once from the Bible, that read personally, but are fundamental rules for all persons.

At the same time, you may identify, which item on anyone of your lists is truly yours, and which did you 'adopt' from another.

Opinions, norms, prejudices, beliefs, and habits are mostly derivatives of your existence in society, they are not necessarily, what you might have come up with if you would live by yourself, on a remote island with only plants, and animals for company.

Bearing in mind that the reason we were

open to outer influence since birth is entirely derived from the fact that Human babies are in need of their caregivers for quite a long time, before we are able to fend for ourselves.

With this thought in mind, compare how Nature equipped animals differently than Humans, for instance, herbivores like horse, goat, and the like can walk and run within minutes of their birth, so they will be able to run away from carnivores eyeing them as 'dinner'.

Fish in the sea are similar. They swim freely from the moment they are born, or spawn.

A Human baby is not even capable of holding neither its head for the first couple of months, or stand, walk, and feed itself for a much longer period.

The need to have caretakers gives birth for the need to learn how to exist within the particular society. It leads the baby to learn from example, and instruction.

Therefore, it is unavoidable that our baby will adopt opinions, conditionings, prejudices, habit, and such. The baby will gage itself against the 'norms' presented to it.

This is why I have likened it all to a heavy

coat.

You are underneath this coat, and in order to define yourself, it will be easier if you will take it off. Taking it off starts with you questioning everything, which constitutes opinions, and belief systems you hold etc.

If you set your premise at the fact that you are unique, and that the only similarity you have to anybody, or anything else in existence, is that you are all 'created' and have the Divine Spark within you, because you are part of Creation – there is nothing outside of Creation.

Being part of Creation grants you also the same rights of existence, the same deserving of being loved, supported, cared for, and appreciated.

Therefore, these should remove from you any apprehension to question yourself.

Imagine questioning yourself to bathing after you have had a mud bath. People used to take mud baths, because they deemed the minerals in the mud to be healing, and healthy for them – and so you may relate to your initial conditioning. Only, you cannot stay covered with mud for the rest of your life, so wash it off!

To help you with unveiling yourself, you

could use the mirror trick whereby, you gaze at yourself in the mirror. Firstly, you will see what you think you look like. Secondly, your inner critic will start voicing its opinions. When you lay your inner critic to rest, you will start seeing what you think other people see 'as you', because they made a point of 'telling' you before. When you let those 'other' off too, you would look, and see someone that you are not sure how to define – you still think you have to define the image, do not be tempted to.

I ask you now to concentrate on your eyes, look 'into' them, beyond their physical characteristics. You do not need 'to do' anything, and certainly *not* to form an opinion.

Your eyes are like deep oceans, vast in size and depth, if you are just courageous enough to 'dive in'.

If you hear any inner opinions, or words, or formed commentaries, you have not yet let go, at this level there should be only silence – a peaceful silence – a quietude that brings relief, and solace.

If you have reached the silence, then you may glimpse the 'formless'. While experiencing the formless, you will come to 'knowing' – do not question that.

This is the point when you would feel that it is so easy to let go of all opinions, beliefs, prejudices, conditionings, habits, and all, which are transient, because you would have met the eternal.

Repeating this mirror trick exercise will embed an inner confidence in you, in the knowing that you are more than just your daily life, and routines.

You would be able to look at your daily life, and exercise the arm's length method, without hurting neither yourself, nor another.

It is at this stage that you may become a far better observer, and therefore will be able to start forming opinions, which are far more true to your own authentic self's nature.

Remember that the eternal within you does not need permanently formed opinions, or beliefs, it only needs you to bask in its peaceful 'being', and while you are about your life in the outer world, always carry with you this feeling, and your observing abilities.

The freedom, granted to you at birth, is found in that 'being state', and it brings forth the power of equipping yourself only with the beliefs, opinions, or habits that are necessary for your survival, growth, and evolution – move with the dance of life, as Life changes from moment to moment.

In reality, no one can, or should, dictate for you what you should believe in, or what tastes you should have. It is within this freedom that you will grow stronger, only make sure that you develop your power of discerning, learning how to 'separate the wheat from the chaff'.

Remember, many things people voice are not necessarily The Truth, it might just be their truth, or just a passing opinion. Weigh what you hear, and all forms of input, as your eternal self knows the Truth.

Unveil From All The Coats - Sing Your Heart

Oh Mirror!

You have been my friend for so long now
Oh Mirror!
From my youth to adulthood always true
Oh Mirror!

As I gazed at you, I knew me well
As you gazed back, we journeyed well
Thank you dear friend, Oh Mirror,
For always being whole & True & Gentle

May our time will offer us many smiles
And the gazing will take us very far
And my dreams will show in your reflection
And golden light will carry them through.

XI
This Which is Success

Success through the ages deemed to be a favourable outcome to an aim or goal alas, this is too singular.

What if instead, we will look for that which could be continuous, multiple and sustained.

When we look at what signifies success, inwardly instead of outwardly, we will see clearly that the person experiencing success has reached harmony and equilibrium with their goal.

My thought that: *"If you believe your destination, you become your goal,* (© 02/11/2004)" allows you to see that the harmony and equilibrium that is reached, is the actual state of being when you unite and align with your destination, so really *your goal is to be one with your destination.*

Then, success is actually a state of being that continuously attests to your unity with that which you 'know' you 'want'. It is almost the same to when you are trying to recall something from your memory, like a name or number. When you keep 'trying' you don't seem to 'get' it, but once you surrender and let go – it suddenly comes to you. Why sometimes things come quickly to you, and sometimes not, and yet, other times the same easy things become hard, and vice versa?

Well, if you think of harmony, as a state of being, you should ask yourself: what does it take to be in this state, or to get to it when you are not in it.

We always ask ourselves that which we would like to remember. We trust that we know it, because we already proved to ourselves previously that we do. We know that it is a question of 'going there' in our memory and 'fetching it'. Thereafter, it is a simple process in our minds.

What if we ask ourselves why recalling seems simple, and getting something we might not have had before isn't. After all, even a thing we ask ourselves to recall had to be learnt first.

A baby doesn't have apprehensions about learning, no matter how easy or hard the process is. An encouraging care-giver may help and/or usher a faster learning, but many a times it has been proven that the spirit of the learner was the most necessary ingredient in the learning, as well as sometimes being the only ingredient.

What if we'll use the analogy of a magnet? When two magnets pull towards each other, or when a magnet pulls towards a material with magnetizing properties, it seems natural to see the attraction.

What if we are the magnets and our wishful destinations are of magnetizing properties, and it is when we exercise our magnetic powers that we draw our destination nearer, towards us.

Therefore, if we ask ourselves what do we truly want, and then we trust that we know that it is for us, then we remove any obstacle standing in our way, which could be anything from a belief system we hold to a wrong company we keep, or wrong habit, or wrong line of thoughts etc.

Thereafter, our 'powers' are purer and will be stronger. If we then keep our 'transmitter' vibrating continuously and strongly, then that which we would like to bring forth to us will be affected more strongly.

Thus, being in a success state of mind requires us to keep all this in mind and exercise it continuously.

Why would a baby have a spontaneous faith without even knowing that he has it? The baby only knows that it is his nature: to evolve, to grow, to advance, and to continue. Only the people in this baby's life teach him to stop, to mistrust and to hesitate thus, delaying or stopping his advancement.

The baby's innate thirst for advancement and independence is inborn growth-ability programmed in his core of being – there is no doubt that it shall happen, only disasters stop it.

Therefore, if we will equate it to success and propose an axiom that success is inborn in us, we may then ask: why and when did we learn that success is unattainable or that it may be attained only if you 'lucky'? And why would the expectations of Human-Beings are usually that Life is suffering and hardship?

A seed germinating in the ground knows its direction towards the fresh air and warm sun. It breathes the minimal air within the soil until it finds his way out to the open. Actually, it does not matter to the seed how soft or hard the soil is – it does find his way out, it does fulfil its innate promise of existence – it is not discouraged in the face of adversity, nor in environmental hardship. A successful seed growing to full capacity – has a good life as its reward. While, a seed that did not withstand the hardship surrendered and rejoined the Whole through the regular transformation of Life – with no devastating sorrow, but with knowing of the continuation of the Life Force.

Thus, if we'd like to simulate the successful seed, we should stand steadfast in our soul's purpose, and navigate our lives while, holding in our mind-eyes the image of our destination, and go on holding onto it, and enriching our faith and our inner drumbeat – march on, and on, and on…

Words like cautiousness, doubtfulness, hesitation and consequences are born of lack of faith that only gives birth to fear.

I am not saying that one should not apply smarts to one's own navigation and choice making, but one must be careful not to create unnecessary delays, those that even cause the light and energy to dissipate enough to leave one with no momentum at all. Even the ship at sea chooses a direction and erects the sails up, so the wind may help it arrive at its destination.

Consequently, what is really asked of us if we choose to make success our basic mind-set, is that we should not let distractions, interruptions and disturbances take much time and energy of us, and certainly not deter our focus-ability.

You see, it is in the loss of time spent on such interruptions that we are leading ourselves away from our destinations, and then we may fall prey to wrong belief system dictating that we lost the opportunity and now, it is too late, or we have become too old, none of which is true.

In taking time off to rest and contemplate, in living a life of a healthy rhythm, rather than haste or urgency, we have the opportunity to re-magnetize ourselves to our destination, like a compass that has to be put stationary, so its magnetic needle may show North.

Then, we have a chance to re-align ourselves to our own north, our soul's purpose, and adjust our vibrational frequency true.

Then, we can let go of our disturbances and live and be. Then in the quiet of our equanimity, we arrive at our success, time and time again.

We only need prove it to ourselves, as we live our own lives, and not somebody else's.

Of course, one must remember that one lives in a society, community, and has needs and obligations, but that does not mean that you have to give yourself up!

All that it means is that while attending to those things, you keep your destination in mind, you live life to the full, and as you know: no man is an island, all to his own.

For an idea to come to fruition or manifestation it needs to be expressed, energy has to be focused upon the detail of its particularity.

The acknowledgement of the idea's uniqueness will bring forth its manifestation or fulfilment.

Unveil From All The Coats - Sing Your Heart

Epilogue

We, The Human Beings on this lovely Earth, succeeded in our evolution, survival, and development mainly in tropical weather areas, and although we wondered also to cold areas, we did not start there.

Therefore, unburden yourself from all the unneeded 'coats', we do not require them.

Set yourself onto the adventure of discovering the vastness of your being, the greatness of your consciousness, and the limitless of your abilities. You would be better off wearing 'light' on this adventure, which may be accomplished by having an open heart at all times.

It reminds me that at one time, a Raccoon came to visit the birdbath I put out, and which I can see through my study's window. He drank the water almost in a longing way. It was unusual, both in mannerism and in the fact that after living in this place for years, that was the first time ever that I have seen a Raccoon there.

I decided to check the Racoon's Wisdom, as it is portrayed in the old wisdom, when I also came across a quote from Ralph Waldo Emerson, which says, "The creation of a thousand forests is in one acorn". The interesting think in it is that apparently, Raccoons like to eat nuts, and the acorn is their most favourite nut.

Can you then imagine if you could see the inner world of a Raccoon, and envisage thousands upon thousands of forests held in his heart?

How vast his existence would be!

How vast our existence is?

Appendices

I.   Assessment

II.   How to get the assessment evaluators

III.   A Word About This Series

Appendix I

How Kind & Helpful I am Towards Myself Assessment

The following is a tool I would like you to use, only as a tool, and not a judge. We all need reference points that allow us to navigate our lives better; this assessment's intention is to give you such reference points, and even some ideas. This will allow you, with repetitive use, to navigate your life in an easier manner hopefully, to happiness and well-being.

Please make a point of re-using it periodically, for example, every 2-3 months, and re-assess you. You are the only one you should answer to, as long as your behaviour is not hurting other. Think of yourself as a growing and developing plant (of your choice) that finds the best way to live well and fulfil the promise within.

I divided the measuring items to the following subjects, and you may draw from them the ideas that might improve your life.

How Kind & Helpful I am Towards Myself:

1. In life style;
2. In my "duties";
3. In my "priorities";
4. In my aspirations / purposes of Life;
5. In my relationships: to myself and to others;
6. In relating to change;
7. In understanding & celebrating myself.

So, here we are, please turn the page and choose a degree of accuracy pertaining to your evaluation of yourself, from 1-5 where, 1 will be the least degree and 5 the most degree.

May this assessment bring you joy and laughter, the encouragement to grow and enjoy your life to the full.

Sincerely Yours,

Please Choose from:				
Least Correct	Maybe So	Most Probably	Feels Good	Absolutely
1	2	3	4	5

How Kind & Helpful I am Towards Myself In life style:

No.	Evaluation	Degree
1	I breathe fresh air everyday	
2	I keep my environment clean	
3	I sleep a minimum of 7 hours and not more than 9 hours	
4	I give myself regular 5 minutes breaks throughout the day, so I'll keep being fresh	
5	I am able to regulate my environmental level of noise	
6	I spend less than 2 hours watching television and/or another electronic device	
7	I remember to eat the correct number of times a day for me	
8	I drink at least 4-8 glasses of fresh water a day	
	Total:	

Continue…

Please Choose from:

Least Correct	Maybe So	Most Probably	Feels Good	Absolutely
1	2	3	4	5

How Kind & Helpful I am Towards Myself In my "duties":

No.	Evaluation	Degree
1	I always remove garbage and recycling items on timely basis	
2	I pay my bills on or before their due date and keep a good standing reference	
3	I file my tax returns on time	
4	I take care of the people who depend on me, as well as myself	
5	I keep my correspondence up-to-date	
6	At work, I focus on work and refrain from surfing the Internet in personal interests	
7	I fulfil my promises to the best of my ability	
8	I am always on time for all of my appointments	
	Total:	

Continue...

Please Choose from:

Least Correct	Maybe So	Most Probably	Feels Good	Absolutely
1	2	3	4	5

How Kind & Helpful I am Towards Myself In my "priorities":

No.	Evaluation	Degree
1	My health and well-being is always first in my priorities, so I'll be there for others too	
2	I always attend to my spiritual nourishment	
3	I attend to my livelihood in earnest, so I truly earn it	
4	I re-examine all my tasks priorities regularly in order to keep a well ordered life	
5	I take time to study and further my knowledge, so I'll keep on growing & advancing	
6	I take time to exercise my body, mind & soul towards an optimum health	
7	Every evening I examine my day and prepare myself for tomorrow	

Continue…

Please Choose from:				
Least Correct	*Maybe So*	*Most Probably*	*Feels Good*	*Absolutely*
1	*2*	*3*	*4*	*5*

8	Every evening I let go of all which is unlike love and that which is not my business	
	Total:	

Continue…

Please Choose from:

Least Correct	Maybe So	Most Probably	Feels Good	Absolutely
1	2	3	4	5

How Kind & Helpful I am Towards Myself In my aspirations / purposes of Life:

No.	Evaluation	Degree
1	I acknowledge that I was born with the right to succeed in life	
2	I research my aspirations & life purposes and intuitively validate them	
3	I take inspired action to follow my life's mission	
4	I study all that is important to help me achieving my aspirations	
5	I act as though I am living my life's purposes even if I cannot prove it yet	
6	I envisage myself as an accomplished person who steps confi-i dently	
7	I am exhilarated to discover life's supportive evidences when I follow my heart	

Continue…

Unveil From All The Coats - Sing Your Heart

Please Choose from:				
Least Correct	*Maybe So*	*Most Probably*	*Feels Good*	*Absolutely*
1	2	3	4	5

8	I keep cool, calm & collected to the best of my ability, so I can listen to my heart	
	Total:	

Continue…

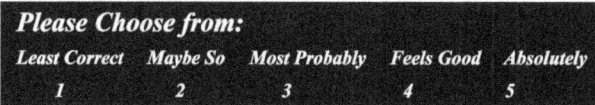

How Kind & Helpful I am Towards Myself In my relationships: to myself and to others:

No.	Evaluation	Degree
1	I always remember that if I am not there for myself, no one else would be	
2	I always remember that the example I give others, they mirror to me	
3	I relate to another as a messenger versus someone who comes to hurt me	
4	I remember that no one can hurt me unless I give them sanction to do so	
5	I help others without sacrificing myself in the process	
6	My intention is to be a gift to life and others, so I refrain from whatever negate it	

Continue…

Please Choose from:				
Least Correct	*Maybe So*	*Most Probably*	*Feels Good*	*Absolutely*
1	2	3	4	5

7	I remember that we're all part of the same creation and deserve love & respect	
8	I regularly work at my graciousness & gentleness towards myself & others	
	Total:	

Continue…

Please Choose from:				
Least Correct	Maybe So	Most Probably	Feels Good	Absolutely
1	2	3	4	5

How Kind & Helpful I am Towards Myself In relating to change:

No.	Evaluation	Degree
1	I always remember that we usher the change for our younger generation	
2	I always remember that I am looked at as an example with my reactions	
3	I enrich my adaptability by nourishing myself body, mind & soul	
4	I am aware that when I feel irritation, I need to examining my reaction to change	
5	I always remember that change is the most natural act of life's transformation	
6	I cultivate excitement to the adventure that change brings	
7	I always draw courage and solace from watching nature's changing nature	

Continue...

Please Choose from:				
Least Correct	Maybe So	Most Probably	Feels Good	Absolutely
1	2	3	4	5

8	I live in a seasonal & cyclical life style and accept it lovingly	
	Total:	

Continue...

Please Choose from:

Least Correct	Maybe So	Most Probably	Feels Good	Absolutely
1	2	3	4	5

How Kind & Helpful I am Towards Myself In understanding & celebrating myself:

No.	Evaluation	Degree
1	I always remember that I am created by the creator in its sanction & love	
2	I understand that I am on a journey of a personal growth	
3	I linger in the moments of compliments and when good things happen to me	
4	I accept my mistakes as reference points of feedback, and move on	
5	I remember my birthday and all dates that promote me	
6	I take time to spend with myself and listen to my inner guidance	
7	I acknowledge that I am the master & creator of my life, and take heed of the results	

Continue…

Please Choose from:				
Least Correct	*Maybe So*	*Most Probably*	*Feels Good*	*Absolutely*
1	*2*	*3*	*4*	*5*

8	I refrain from reacting by taking a deep breath and re-think my response	
	Total:	

Well Done!

When we'll meet again, we'll check the totals and see where you stand, or look at the next Appendix for the details how to get the evaluation details from me.

Continue...

Appendix II

> Life Coaching for your
> 　　　　　Personal Growth and Validity.
> Enhancing your
> 　　Humanity and strengthening your gift to Life,
> 　and also helping you to know that Life is a Gift.
> Broadening your
> 　　　　　outlook of Life and your power within it.
>
> 　　　　　　　　　　　　　　　　　　　TF

Do you know?

In days gone by, in societies that were more united and concerned with survival, people of all ages and genders were encouraged to be the best that they can be, so their contributions to the society made a major difference to the level of survival achieved. Each person counted. Each person mattered. Each person was either an asset or a liability.

The number of people/members in these societies was low, as per today's terms.

Alas, today we are many more. Today, our societies are so large that we hardly know each other.

That is not to say that we have changed the most important fundamentals namely, each person is response-able for themselves. Each person has the power of choice and Free Will therefore, you have to make your own choices while thinking of your highest good and the highest good of all.

Think how wonderful it could be if all the members of our societies will be happy, will feel powerful, because they would know that they stand tall, and no one can belittle or control them.

Life coaching can help us move forward in that direction.

In order to receive the actual Evaluation Score, feel free to contact me via:

http://www.experientialelixir.ca

and/or using the email:

coach@experientialelixir.ca

I would be very happy to give you this score, and spend free 15 minutes discussing it.

Awaiting your call & wishing you All The Best.

A word about this series

In this busy day and age, where people have more input than they sometimes able to concentrate on, I venture to offer a more succinct manner of dealing with subjects of interest, or need.

The image of a tip of an iceberg immediately brings to mind that there is much more unseen, underwater if you may.

Consciousness is very much like the waters of a vast sea whereby, our conscious thoughts are those that exist above the water level, and our submerged portion of the conscious – is very much our unknown part therefore, many times, it is called the sub-conscious, or the unconscious.

Our feelings are just the waves, and wave crests, which are created by the winds of time, and occurrences of life upon the surface.

I would like to have your brief time of contemplation in reading this short book yet, to impress your mind with a profound message, and content.

It is in the succinct that we may never be overwhelmed, and in overpowering vast amount of input that we are fatigued.

I trust you know that much more could have been said about the subject of the book, but maybe what was said is enough.

I wish you joy and peace – always.

Notes

Notes

Notes

Notes

Notes

Notes

Notes

Notes

Notes

Notes

www.ingramcontent.com/pod-product-compliance
Lightning Source LLC
Chambersburg PA
CBHW031407160426
43196CB00007B/932